Tony Harrison
Palladas : Poems

Anvil Press Poetry

First published in 1975
Second edition published in 1984
by Anvil Press Poetry Ltd
69 King George Street London SE10 8PX

ISBN 0 85646 127 X

This book is published
with financial assistance from
The Arts Council of Great Britain

Photoset in Baskerville
by Katerprint Co Ltd, Oxford
and printed in England
at The Arc & Throstle Press
Todmorden Lancs

POETICA 5
Palladas: Poems

Poetica is a series of texts, translations
and miscellaneous works related to poetry.

Editor: Peter Jay
Advisory editors: Michael Hamburger,
Peter Levi, Betty Radice and Peter Whigham

by Tony Harrison

POETRY

Earthworks, 1964
Newcastle is Peru, 1969
The Loiners, 1970
Palladas: Poems, 1975
from The School of Eloquence
  and other poems, 1978
A Kumquat for John Keats, 1981
U.S. Martial, 1981
Continuous, 1981
Selected Poems, 1984

THEATRE

Aikin Mata (with James Simmons), 1966
The Misanthrope, 1973
Phaedra Britannica, 1975
Bow Down, 1977
The Passion, 1977
The Bartered Bride, 1978
The Oresteia, 1981

Palladas haunted Harrison:
These versions of yours! God!
What did I ever do to you
you rotten little sod?

ACKNOWLEDGEMENTS

Some of these versions first appeared in *The Greek Anthology* edited by Peter Jay (Allen Lane, 1973; Penguin Books, 1981) and in *Phoenix*.

The translator wishes to acknowledge the assistance of the Arts Council of Great Britain.

PREFACE

ONE OF THE DISADVANTAGES of the traditional organization of those 4,000-odd epigrams that make up the Greek Anthology is that the poems are arranged according to subject matter and type, thus obscuring the singularity of individual poets. Peter Jay's decision to rearrange the poems by poet and period for his selection of modern versions allowed distinctive talents to emerge clearly from the welter of reiterated themes; among the most notable of them, that gloomy epigrammatist of the fourth century AD, Palladas of Alexandria.

Gilbert Highet places Palladas among the world's great pessimists – with Juvenal, Swift, Nietzsche, Bernard de Morval (the author of *De Contemptu Mundi*) and Ecclesiastes; while J. W. Mackail, somewhat tantalizingly, as he felt unable actually to print the poem in his selection, regards poem 1, sometimes known as 'The Descent of Man', as 'one of the most mordant sarcasms ever passed upon Mankind.' His dates are usually given as AD 360–430 but C. M. Bowra in an essay 'Palladas and the Christians' (reprinted in *On Greek Margins*) argues fairly plausibly for putting his birth at about 319, and – since we know from poem 40 (see also my note) that he lived at least seventy-two years – for placing his death around the end of the century. This would make him an old man at the time of the savage anti-Pagan riots and destruction of Greek temples, the looting and burning of Pagan objects of worship by Christian mobs given licence by the edicts of the Emperor Theodosius in 391, and inflamed by the rabble-rousing Bishop Theophilus. That his last years should have coincided with the virtual destruction of the system of beliefs to which he owed his always precarious living as a schoolmaster, gives us an added insight into the bitter force of his poetry. The new dates calculated by Bowra also mean that he died before he could witness the dreadful murder of the Hellenistic teacher and intellectual Hypatia whose flesh was scraped from her bones by Christians wielding oyster shells like razors. But there is no doubt that he must have witnessed similar events, even though the well-known poem 18 seems to me more gnomic than specifically about the persecution of non-Christians. I have included the poem (67) which Palladas was supposed to have addressed to Hypatia since their two names, the martyr of Hellenistic culture and the poet of its last exasperated gasp, have been traditionally associated in the drama of its extinction.

Palladas, when noticed at all, is generally regarded as the last poet of Paganism, and it is in this role that I have sought to present a consistent dramatic personality in this selection of slightly less than half the poems ascribed to him in the Greek Anthology. His are the last hopeless blasts of the old Hellenistic world, giving way reluctantly, but without much resistance, before the cataclysm of Christianity. It is difficult if not impossible at this time of sectarian violence, Pagan hopelessness and Christian barbarity, to characterize Hellenism as worldly sanity, or Christianity as sweetness and light. Poor Palladas seems to be in the predicament of his murderer in that rather nasty poem 'The Murderer & Sarapis' (70). There seems to have been little or no moral sustenance or sense of identity left in the one, and little sense of hope in the other. The choice was between a crumbled past and a future of specious regeneration. This is the conflict of the following rather mysterious poem of his (Greek Anthology 10.82) about the Christian attitude to the Hellenes:

> We non-Christians are dead, and only seem
> alive; the life we're living's a bad dream;

8

or so THEY say. My version of it's this:
we're alive but wonder if life is!

The irony of Palladas's image as 'the last of the Pagans' gloomily watching the Christian world-view assert itself, even, as I have imagined, in the person of his own wife (see poem 52), is that his is a Paganism so turned in on itself that in its hatred of life and the senses, and its scorn of worldly goods and endowments, it seems very like the spirit of early Christianity; 'a Father of the Church' Palladas has been called, 'who has all the proper characteristics except faith, hope and charity.'

His bitterness is compounded of historical pessimism, the poverty of a poor teacher dependent on rich Hellenes for his very precarious existence (see poem 31), and a bad marriage which seems to have led to general misogyny. His ironic poems (such as 63–65) on the new time-serving roles of the old gods show that bitter sense of humour which prevents a man from toppling over into the abyss of his own creation. There is no sense of joy in his few poems on the *carpe diem* theme. He recommends drink as oblivion. The sense of death is stronger than any urge to sensual life. The tone of his bitterness ranges from common-room bitchiness (e.g. poem 37), still so much a part of the 'humanist' tradition, the donnish *moue* and pedantic repartee, to a cosmic derision like an orchestrated death-rattle. What is unique and even invigorating about Palladas is that there is no sense at all of 'gracious' surrender either to the inevitability of death or to historical change. Even the fatalism of poems like 10 seems grudging. If there is only the bleakest of Epicurean attitudes, there is certainly nothing Stoical about Palladas. He is one of those embarrassing but heroic figures who are not dignified in despair, refusing to be noble on the gallows or to make peace with their maker. It is perhaps this aspect of his tone, his 'raging

9

against the dying of the light', that makes commentators like Mackail refer to his 'harsh thought and half barbarous language' or like Gilbert Highet to regret his lack of 'great verbal dexterity'. He is certainly not elegant (and most certainly not in that false sense often wished on to the classics by classicists); his is not the stylish after-dinner despair of the high table, the sighing gestures of surfeit, but the authentic snarl of a man trapped physically in poverty and persecution, and metaphysically in a deep sense of the futile. He is not, as it happens, incapable of the dexterous play on words, the pedantic pun or the neat turn (e.g. poem 51). For all his complaints about life as a *grammatikos* teaching children to learn Homer by rote, he must have been familiar enough with the Greek traditions to have produced any amount of passably smooth imitations, and so we must assume that the undeniable roughness of his tone was worked for. His epigrams are much more 'pointed' than most of his predecessors' in the Greek Anthology, and 'point' is somehow the formal equivalent of despair. There is a strong sense of form in Palladas and it is something which barely seems able to contain the apoplectic energy of his nihilistic scorn. It is as if the formal endeavour and metrical tension were all that stood between Palladas and choking silence, sheer cosmic exasperation and what Beckett's Lucky calls 'divine aphasia'.

T. H.
Gregynog,
March 1974

Palladas : Poems

I

Think of your conception, you'll soon forget
what Plato puffs you up with, all that
'immortality' and 'divine life' stuff.

Man, why dost thou think of Heaven? Nay
consider thine origins in common clay

's one way of putting it but not blunt enough.

Think of your father, sweating, drooling, drunk,
you, his spark of lust, his spurt of spunk.

2

Ignorant of all logic and all law
Fortune follows her own blind course,
kind to the criminal, trampling on the just,
flaunting her irrational, brute force.

3

Life's a performance. Either join in
lightheartedly, or thole the pain.

4

Born naked. Buried naked. So why fuss?
All life leads to that first nakedness.

5

Born crying, and after crying, die.
It seems the life of man's just one long cry.

Pitiful and weak and full of tears,
Man shows his face on earth and disappears.

6

Our nostrils snuffle life from delicate air.
We turn our faces to the sun's bright glare,
organs that get their life out of a breeze.
Give our windpipes just one stiffish squeeze,
life's gone, we're brought down low to death.

We're puff and bluster cut off with one press,
utter nothings, sustained by nothingness
browsing the thin air for our life-breath.

7

Why this desperation to move heaven and earth
to try to change what's doled out at your birth,
the lot you're made a slave to by the gods?

Learn to love tranquillity, and against all odds
coax your glum spirit to its share of mirth.

8

Man's clay, and such a measly bit
and measuring the Infinite!

Leave geography alone, you can't survey
the paltry area of that poor clay.

Forget the spheres and first assess
not space but your own littleness.

9

Agony comes from brooding about death.
   Once dead, a man's spared all that pain.

Weeping for the dead's a waste of breath—
   they're lucky, *they* can't die again.

10

If gale-force Fortune sweeps you off your feet,
  let it; ride it; and admit defeat.

There's no point in resisting; it's too strong—
  willy-nilly, you'll get swept along.

11

Death's a debt that everybody owes,
and if you'll last the night out no-one knows.

Learn your lesson then, and thank your stars
for wine and company and all-night bars.

Life careers gravewards at a breakneck rate,
so drink and love, and leave the rest to Fate.

12

Don't fash yourself, man! Don't complain.
Compared with those dark vastnesses before
and after, life's too brief to be a bore
and you'll never pass this way again.

So until the day you're in your grave
and inevitably you become an incubator
for the new-born worms, don't you behave
as though damned here and now, as well as later.

13

Each new daybreak we are born again.

All our life till now has flown away.

What we did yesterday's already gone.

All we have left of life begins today.

Old men, don't complain of all your years.
Those that have vanished are no longer yours!

14

Life's an ocean-crossing where winds howl
and the wild sea comes at us wave after wave.

With Fortune our pilot, weather fair or foul,
all alike drop anchor in the grave.

15

God's philosophical and so can wait
for the blasphemer and the reprobate—

He calmly chalks their crimes up on His slate.

16

God rot the guts and the guts' indulgences.
It's their fault that sobriety lets go.

17

Observe decorum in your grief. First drink and eat.
Remember Homer's:
>*Guts grieve for nothing but more food.*

Remember his Niobe, burying her butchered brood,
all twelve children, with her mind on meat.

18

Death feeds us up, keeps an eye on our weight
and herds us like pigs through the abattoir gate.

19

Loving the rituals that keep men close,
Nature created means for friends apart:

pen, paper, ink, the alphabet,
signs for the distant and disconsolate heart.

20

Hope! Fortune! *Je m'en fous!*
Both cheats, but I've come through.

Penniless but free, I can ignore
wealth that looks down on the poor.

21

Shun the rich, they're shameless sods
strutting about like little gods,

loathing poverty, the soul
of temperance and self-control.

22

When you start sneering it's not me
you're sneering at, it's poverty.

If he'd been poor and human, Zeus
'd've suffered from the same abuse.

23

Yes, I'm poor. What's wrong with that?
What is it that I've done to earn your hate?

It's not my character you're sneering at,
only the usual senselessness of Fate.

24

Just look at them, the shameless well-to-do
and stop feeling sorry you're without a sou.

25

It's no great step for a poor man to the grave.
    He's lived his life out only half-alive.

But when the man of plenty nears the end of his,
    Death yawns beneath him like a precipice.

26

So, Mister Moneybags, you're loaded? So?
You'll never take it with you when you go.

You've made your pile, but squandered time. Grown old
you can't gloat over age like hoarded gold.

27

Totting up the takings, quick Death can
reckon much faster than the businessman,

who, balancing, blacks out for ever, still
with the total ringing on the till.

28

Racing, reckoning fingers flick
at the abacus. Death's double-quick
comptometer works out the sums.

The stiffening digits, the rigid thumbs
still the clicking. Each bead slides,
like a soul passing over, to the debit side.

29

Poor devil that I am, being so attacked
by wrath in fiction, wrath in fact.

Victim of wrath in literature and life:

1. The *Iliad* and 2. the wife!

30

Grammar commences with a 5-line curse:
Wrath's first and *fatal*'s second verse;
then *sufferings*. The third verse sends
many men to various and violent ends,
and then the fourth and fifth expose
men to Zeus's anger, dogs and crows.

Sad study, grammar! Its whole content's
one long string of accidents!

31

It's grammarians that the gods torment
and Homer's *fatal wrath* 's their instrument.

Monthly (if that!) the grudging nanny wraps
their measly pittance in papyrus scraps.
She nicks some, switches coins, and not content
holds out her grasping claws for 10%,
then lays at teacher's feet a screw of stuff
like paper poppies on a cenotaph.

Just get one loving father to agree
to pay (in decent gold!) a *yearly* fee,
the eleventh month, just when it's almost due,
he'll hire a 'better teacher' and fire you.

Your food and lodging gone, he's got the gall
to crack after-dinner jokes about it all.

32

Nouns *and* poor grammarians decline.
I'm selling off these rotten books of mine,
my Pindar, my Callimachus, the lot.
I'm a bad 'case'. It's poverty I've got.
Dorotheus has given me the sack
and slanders me behind my back.

Help me, Theon, or all that'll stand
between poverty and me's an &

33

Poor little donkey! It's no joke
being a pedant's not a rich man's moke
preened in the palace of the alabarch.

Exist on all the *carets* that I mark
in pupils' proses, little donkey, stay
with me patiently until the day
I get my (patience's first morpheme) pay.

34

This is my mule, a poor long-suffering hack
  with iambic front legs and trochaic back.

Backwards or forwards, he'll take you home
  both ways together like a palindrome.

35

I need mulled wine. Mull? Mull?
O your etymology's a load of bull!

I don't care if it is the Hebrides,
all I need is more mulled vino, *please*.

Old Norse, Gaelic or Teutonic,
it's still a first-rate stomach tonic.

You fetch the lexicon. Mull! Schmull!
Stuff etymology, when my cup's full.

36

A grammarian's daughter had a man
then bore a child m. f. & n.

37

You brainless bastard! O you stupid runt!
Such showing off and you so ignorant!
When the talk's linguistics, you look bored;
your specialism's Plato. Bloody fraud!
Someone says 'Ah, Plato!' then you duck
behind some weighty new phonetics book.

Linguistics! Plato Studies! Dodge and switch,
you haven't a clue, though, which is which.

38

The ignorant man does well to shut his trap
and hide his opinions like a dose of clap.

39

Menander's right, and thought's most fertile soil
　's serendipity, not midnight oil.

40

A lifetime's teaching grammar come to this—
　returned as member for Necropolis!

41 *On Gessius*

i

Fate didn't hustle Gessius to his death.
He ran there well before it, out of breath.

ii

A mortal's better off not deified
or arrogantly over-elevated.

Look at Gessius, always dissatisfied,
puffed up first, and then deflated.

iii

Two crystal-gazers gazed and prophesied
a consulate for Gessius. There wasn't and he died.

Mankind, self-destructive, puffed up with vanities,
even Death itself can't put you wise.

iv

Neglect of *Nothing in excess*
landed Gessius in this pretty mess.
Erudite he may be but a loon
thinking he could reach the moon.
Bellerophon spurred his mount too far
to learn what heavenly bodies are;
he had youth and strength, and he was on
winged Pegasus, was Bellerophon.

Gessius has nothing. Poor Gessius, I fear
hasn't the energy for diarrhoea!

The politician's elephantine conk's
amazing, amazing too the voice that honks
through blubber lips (1 lb. net each)
spouting his loud, ear-shattering speech.

43

Where's the public good in what you write,
raking it in from all that shameless shite,

hawking iambics like so much *Betterbrite?*

44

Better the hangman's noose than surgeon's knife.
The executioner takes life for life
in legalized hatred for those who kill—

the surgeon does you in and sends a bill!

45

There's that old saying: *Ex-domestics can't
run houses of their own.* My equivalent

's: *An advocate's no judge* though he's
as great a pleader as Isocrates.

Those who sell eloquence like common whores
'll foul pure Justice with their dirty paws.

46

𝔐ein 𝔅reast, mein 𝔔orset und mein 𝔏egs
𝔍a dedicates to 𝔍uice like all gut 𝔊riegs.

47

I was promised a horse but what I got instead
was a tail, with a horse hung from it almost dead.

48

Thanks for the haggis. Could you really spare
such a huge bladder so full of air?

49

When you send out invitations, don't ask me.
It's rare fillets that I like not filigree.
A piece of pumpkin each! The table creaks
not with the weight of food but your antiques.

Save your *soirées* for connoisseurs who'll notch
their belts in tighter for a chance to watch
the long procession of your silverware,
for art's sake happy just to starve and stare,
and, for some fine piece to goggle at, forego
all hope of eating, if the hallmarks show.

50

You invite me out, but if I can't attend
I've had the honour and I'm more your friend.

The heart's no gourmet, no, it feels
honour stays hunger more than meals.

51

women all
cause rue

but can be nice
on   occasional

moments   two
to   be   precise

in   bed

& dead

52

Cuckolded husbands have no certain sign
that trusted wives are treacherous, *like mine*.
The ugly woman's not *de facto* pure,
nor every beauty fast. You're never sure.
The beddable girl, though every bidder woos
with cash and comfort's likely to refuse.
There's many a plain nympho who bestows
expensive gifts on all her gigolos.

The serious woman, seemingly man-shy
and never smiling, does that mean chastity?
Such gravity's worn only out of doors;
at home, in secret, they're all utter whores.
The chatty woman with a word for all
may well be chaste, though that's improbable.
Even old age gets goaded into lust;
senility's no guarantee. What can we trust?

I've got twelve gods to swear my honour by,
she, convenient Christianity!

53

The theft of fire. Man's worst bargain yet.
Zeus created Woman, He was that upset!

A woman desiccates a man with cares
and soon gives golden youth his first grey hairs.

But Zeus's married life in Heaven above
's no cloudy mattress of ambrosial love.

Zeus with Hera of the golden throne
longs to be divorced and on His own.

He often has to shove Her from the sky
to a dog-house cumulus to sulk and cry.

Homer knew this well and shows the two
squabbling on Olympus as mere mortals do.

Thus a woman nags and haggles though she lies
beside the Deity of Deities.

54

Man stole fire, and Zeus created flame
much fiercer still. Woman was its name.

Fire's soon put out, but women blaze
like volcanic conflagrations all our days.

55

The women all shout after me and mock:
Look in the mirror, you decrepit wreck!
But I'm too near the end to give a toss
for trivia like grey temples and hair-loss.

A nice, fresh deodorant, some after-shave
for banishing the bad smell of the grave,
a few bright flowers in my falling hair,
a good night's drinking, and I just don't care.

56

When he comes up to the bedroom
and switches on the light,
the poor man with the ugly wife
stares out into the night.

57

Zeus isn't such a raving Casanova
if he's seen this girl and passed her over.

No galloping bull or strong-winged giant swan
to get his hands on this proud courtesan,

who's Leda, Europa, Danaë all rolled
into one, worth ten showers of his gold.

Are courtesans too common to seduce
and only royal virgins fit for Zeus?

58

From Alexandria to Antioch.
From Syria to Italy: no luck!

Between the Tiber and the Nile
not one man to lead you up the aisle.

'Hope springs eternal . . .' though. Good luck, my dear,
husband-hunting through the Gazetteer.

59

With a son called Eros and a wife whose name
's Aphrodite, no wonder that you're lame!

60

Mere ants and gnats and trivia with stings
vent their aggression like all living things,
but you, you think that *I* ought to be meek,
lay myself open, 'turn the other cheek',
not even verbal comebacks, but stay dumb
and choking on my gag till Kingdom Come!

61

Boast you don't obey the wife, I'll say that's balls.
You're a man aren't you, and not a rock or log?
You suffer too. You know what bugs us all's
being the husband and the underdog.

But say: *She doesn't slipper me or sleep around;
no turning a blind eye*, then, *if* that's true,
your bondage isn't bad, being only bound
to one who's chaste and not *too* hard on you.

62

A drink to drown my sorrows and restart
the circulation to my frozen heart!

63 *On a Temple of Fortune Turned into a Tavern*

i

Agh, the world's gone all to fuck
when Luck herself's run out of luck!

ii

Fortune, fortune-maker/breaker,
human nature cocktail-shaker,

goddess once, and now a barmaid
's not too drastic change of trade!

You'll do nicely where you are
behind the counter of *The Fortune Bar*,

metamorphosed to 'mine host'
the character that suits you most.

iii

Fortune, can you hear them making fun,
all the mortals, now you're one?

This time you've really gone too far
blotting out your own bright star.

Once queen of a temple, now you're old
you serve hot toddies to keep out the cold.

Well might you complain, now even you
suffer from yourself as mere men do.

64

The blacksmith's quite a logical man
to melt an Eros down and turn
the God of Love into a frying pan,
something that can also burn.

65

Knocked off his pedestal! THEY've
done *this* to Heracles?
Flabbergasted I began to rave
and went down on my knees:

Giant, whose birth took three whole days,
whose image stands at each crossroad,
you to whom the whole world prays,
our Champion, K.O.ed?

That night he stood at my bed-end
and smiled and said: *I can't complain.*
The winds of change are blowing, friend,
your god's a weather-vane.

66 *Marina's House*

'Baptized' Olympians live here in peace,
spared Treasury furnace and coiner's mould,
the fires of revolution and small change.

67 *Hypatia*

Searching the zodiac, gazing on Virgo,
knowing your province is really the heavens,
finding your brilliance everywhere I look,
I render you homage, revered Hypatia,
teaching's bright star, unblemished, undimmed.

68 *On Monks*

Solitaries? I wonder whether
real solitaries live together?

Crowds of recluses ? Pseuds,
pooling all their 'solitudes'.

A Spartan lad fled from the war.
He didn't want no bullet.
He isn't home two ticks before
his mam's dagger's at his gullet.

She prods him with her stiletto blade
and pricks his yeller belly:
What, a son of mine afraid?
yer spineless little jelly.

If you're allowed to stay alive,
you miserable little crumb,
think how your rotten coward's skive
brings shame on your old mum.

That's if you don't die. If you do
'A mum's a proper martyr'
's what they'll say, but (she ran him through)
no shame for me or Sparta.

A murderer spread his palliasse
beneath a rotten wall
and in his dream came Sarapis
and warned him it would fall:

Jump for your life, wretch, and be quick!
One more second and you're dead.
He jumped and tons of crumbling brick
came crashing on his bed.

The murderer gasped with relief,
he thanked the gods above.
It was his innocent belief
they'd saved him out of love.

But once again came Sarapis
in the middle of the night,
and once more uttered prophecies
that set the matter right:

Don't think the gods have let you go
and connive at homicide.
We've spared you that quick crushing, so
we can get you crucified.

NOTES

poem

17 NIOBE – daughter of Tantalus, wife of Amphion of Thebes, who bragged to the goddess Leto that whereas the goddess had only borne twins (Apollo and Artemis), she had borne many children. According to the tragedians there were seven sons and seven daughters, but Homer (*Iliad* xxiv.601) gives her six of each. Apollo slew the sons, and Artemis the daughters.

29–31 Palladas was a *grammatikos*, a sort of secondary teacher who taught pupils to commit to memory as much of Homer as possible. The point of these three poems depends on that fact and on the opening lines of the *Iliad*, which read in Dryden's translation:

The Wrath of *Peleus* Son, O Muse, resound;
Whose dire Effects the *Grecian* Army found:
And many a Heroe, King, and hardy Knight,
Were sent, in early Youth, to Shades of Night:
Their Limbs a Prey to Dogs and Vultures made;
So was the Sov'reign Will of *Jove* obey'd.

32 THEON – the protector Palladas addresses himself to was one of the chief scholars of his day, whose work on astronomy is praised in an epigram and who is sometimes said to be represented by two poems of his own in the Greek Anthology. Hypatia, celebrated in another poem often ascribed to Palladas (see on 67, below), was Theon's daughter.

33–35 The puns in the Greek of these poems cannot be reproduced but I have tried to create equivalent pedantic little jokes to show this side of the man.

33 The 'alabarch' was the chief magistrate of the Jews at Alexandria.

44

35 This poem depends in the original on the word *konditon* (from the Latin 'vinum conditum'), which is wine spiced with honey and pepper. Hence my Mull. I have taken the joke to be rather like Mr Squeers' Educational System in Dotheboys Hall.

40 The poem begins literally, 'Having lived a pound of years . . .', i.e. 'at the age of seventy-two', there being seventy-two *solidi* in the gold pound of Constantine.

46 A Gothic soldier copies the behaviour of his Greek comrades, his knowledge of the language presumably limited to a few truncated words of command from his sergeant-major.

52 I have imagined as a dramatic solution to the last lines of this poem that Palladas had a wife who not only flirted with other men but also with the tenets of Christianity, thereby cancelling the vows she made under pagan rites to her husband. This is also why in poem 60 the wife is made to quote the explicitly Christian injunction 'turn the other cheek'. Remembering that Palladas witnessed the Christian violence against non-Christians and their institutions in AD 391, his splenetic derision at this piece of wifely proselytization is understandable.

57 ZEUS had a talent for metamorphosis which he used to seduce mortal women: Leda (as a swan), Europa (as a bull) and Danaë (as a shower of gold).

59 HEPHAISTOS (Vulcan), the god of fire, was lame in one foot.

65 THEY are, of course, the Christian pillagers.

66 For a discussion of this poem see C. M. Bowra, 'Palladas and the Converted Olympians' in *On Greek Margins* (1970), pp. 245–52.

67 There are doubts that this poem is by Palladas (see G. Luck, *Harvard Studies in Classical Philology* lxiii, 1958, pp. 462–6). Hypatia was the daughter of the astronomer-mathematician Theon (see above on 32)

and was renowned for her elucidations of the geometry of Apollonius and Diophantus and for her public teaching of the philosophy of Plato and Aristotle. Her death at the hands of Christians is described in Gibbon, *The Decline and Fall of the Roman Empire*, chapter 47:

'Hypatia was torn from her chariot, stripped naked, dragged to the church, and inhumanly butchered by the hands of Peter the reader and a troop of savage and merciless fanatics: her flesh was scraped from her bones with sharp oyster shells, and her quivering limbs were delivered to the flames.'

70 SARAPIS (or Serapis) was an Egyptian god with a thriving cult at Alexandria. A temple of Sarapis, said to be a very rich one, was among those destroyed by Christian mobs in AD 391. The god was always said to appear to devotees in dreams.

REFERENCES

This table gives references to the book and poem number of the poems as traditionally assembled in the Greek Anthology. The most accessible text is W. R. Paton's *The Greek Anthology* (1916; five volumes) in the Loeb series. The epigraph on page 5 is after Palladas' poem 11.263.

1 — 10.45	26 — 10.60	48 — 9.486
2 — 10.62	27 — 11.289	49 — 11.371
3 — 10.72	28 — 11.290	50 — 9.176
4 — 10.58	29 — 9.168	51 — 11.381
5 — 10.84	30 — 9.173	52 — 10.56
6 — 10.75	31 — 9.174	53 — 9.165
7 — 10.77	32 — 9.175	54 — 9.167
8 — 11.349	33 — 11.383	55 — 11.54
9 — 10.59	34 — 11.317	56 — 11.287
10 — 10.73	35 — 9.502	57 — 5.257
11 — 11.62	36 — 9.489	58 — 11.306
12 — 10.78	37 — 11.305	59 — 11.307
13 — 10.79	38 — 10.98	60 — 10.49
14 — 10.65	39 — 10.52	61 — 10.55
15 — 10.94	40 — 10.97	62 — 11.55
16 — 10.57	41 — 7.682	63 — 9.180
17 — 10.47	7.684	9.181
18 — 10.85	7.688	9.183
19 — 9.401	7.683	64 — 9.773
20 — 9.172	42 — 11.204	65 — 9.441
21 — 10.61	43 — 11.291	66 — 9.528
22 — 11.302	44 — 11.280	67 — 9.400
23 — 11.303	45 — 10.48	68 — 11.384
24 — 10.93	46 — 6.85	69 — 9.397
25 — 10.63	47 — 11.293	70 — 9.378

POETICA